LABOR
THE TESTIMONY OF TED GALL

LABOR
THE TESTIMONY OF TED GALL

Poems by
Cecilia Woloch

Accents Publishing • Lexington, Kentucky • 2024

Printed in the United States of America

Accents Publishing
Editor: Katerina Stoykova
Cover Image: Ted Gall at age 14, Gall family archive

ISBN: 978-1-961127-12-8
First Edition

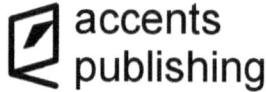

Accents Publishing is an independent press for brilliant voices. For a catalog of current and upcoming titles, please visit us on the Web at

www.accents-publishing.com

CONTENTS

I. MINING (1918–1920s)

You had to load 20 ton out of there.

That was for your shift.
Then you had at least 5 ton of stuff
that you threw away
that was no good
and maybe about 10 ton that you got paid for
if you were lucky.

Then your 30 cents a ton made you $3.80 per day
and then you had to pay for rent on your lamp
and buy your powder.

Of course, you had a lot of work that was called dead-work
that you gave to them—
putting up support poles, dynamiting, etc....
That was for free. You only got paid
for the tonnage that crossed the scales.
Then you usually had guys down there
that would cheat on the scales.

You were lucky if you ended up with a dollar a day.

❧

We got ventilation from big fans on top of the mines
that would blow air down.
You had two places:
one was the hole where the men went down
and the other the hole where the coal came out.

And usually the air went down the hole where the men went in
where the cages went up and down.

You could always tell when the air wasn't circulating
because where the men were working
there was just a cloud of steam.

❧

If you had your car full loaded
and you were waiting for the motorman to come
and bring you an empty one
and take your full one away
then you would have a sandwich or something.
Then as soon as you got your car
you would hurry to get it loaded.
The motorman comes and goes
and if you're not loaded, he'll go and leave you
and then you miss a trip.

They had it all planned out
so they had just enough cars in there
for you to load your cut out.

After they had the machine coal taken out
then they had the pick men who would follow them
where it was too dangerous any more
to go back in with the machine.

Then the pick men would go in there and hit the face.
If you just hit the face with your pick
the coal would just fly out because of the squeeze on it.
Then you worked like mad.
When you're doing the pick work
you can hear that limestone cracking up there above you.

Boundaries were set by the engineers.
Lots of times mistakes were made.
For instance, a mine was worked out.
It would gradually fill with water.
Sometimes the weight of the water
would just push that coal right out of there.
Then you were in trouble.
Most falls happen just (snap) like that.

The company, even if they knew they had a bad roof,
wouldn't do anything about it
until they had a fall.
Then they only took care of the effects.

Prevention, that was something else again.
That they didn't do
because that took money.

Now, in Rural Ridge, the town next to Russellton,
going down toward the river by the turnpike,
they had a fall. A man was caught under it
and they had mules in the mine
to move the cars around
and a mule was caught in the fall, too.
There was a lot of screaming and commotion
and the men working in the other room heard it
and came over to where the fall was.

The boss, he was sitting on the mule's head
to try to keep it from thrashing around.
Now the first man that got over there,
the boss told him to sit on the mule's head
and to hold that mule's head down.
This old Polish man said, "Shit on you,
that man over there is under stuff."

The Polish man was fired
because he wanted to help the man under the fall
instead of sitting on the mule's head.

A mule cost money
and they could always hire another man.

&

II. UNIONS (1920s–1930s)

All the Gall boys worked in the mines.
I went to work when I was twelve years old
driving the mules.
That was 1918.
There was a shortage of workers then
because all the fellows were in the service.
But as soon as the war was over
and the older fellows returned
then the kids weren't wanted anymore.

In Russellton, if you didn't have someone
to get you into a mine or a job
then you had to go to some relations
somewhere like Detroit.

I didn't go to any relations.
I went in the Army. I was fourteen.
It was an escape. It was the way out
because otherwise there was nothing.
There was nothing there.

After a year in the Army
and four years in the Marines
I came back to Russellton
and went to work in the mines.

&

We had to strike for better conditions.
We had to strike every step of the way.
John L. Lewis and those guys got big names
but any progress that was made
was made over them and in spite of them.
They were getting good wages.
They were getting good salaries
from the dues that were paid by the miners.
They didn't want that disrupted.
They had a working agreement with the coal companies
and everything went along real fine for them.
If you wanted any progress at all
it was only through wildcat strikes.

⁊

During the '27 strike
when people were being evicted out of their houses
my brother Ervin was building barracks
for the evicted people to live in.
The company didn't like this.
The company owned the houses
so they could evict people if they didn't work.
They wanted workers to have no place to go.
They wanted them to have nothing
so they would just acquiesce.

Because of the strike, I got away from the mines
and it wasn't until November 1928 that I went back.
I guess I was desperate. You just couldn't get a job.
I had been really sick with the flu in February '28
when we were all really sick with it
and Ervin died from it.

≈

And then Roosevelt came in
and then you were allowed to organize for unions again.

But the company had people
who would tell the bosses what was going on.
They maneuvered a fellow to work with me.
He was telling the company everywhere I went
and almost my thoughts.

The Coal and Iron Police,
they controlled all the roads around the coal camps.

I went into Butler County to organize there.
I didn't even have one contact to talk to.
I would go and wait alongside the road
when the people came out from work.
I would walk alongside them and talk to them
as they were walking home.
They were frightened. They were afraid to talk to anyone
for fear that someone would report them to the company.

At Russellton, after we had reorganized there
and had a semblance of a union,
we had no way of collecting dues
and had no contract with the company.
Everything was more or less freewill.

Good fellows, strong fellows—
mentally, morally, every way strong fellows
but they were frightened.
We had to collect dues out on the road,
on the public road.
They would drop their dues money on the ground

and then walk across the road to the other side
so that they wouldn't even be seen talking to us.

But we succeeded, we succeeded.

Our fight was not only against the company
but also against the hierarchy that was running the union.
Everything was stacked against the workers.
The Republican party and the Democratic party,
they were run by the hierarchy of the union officials
and the coal company bosses and owners.
We had to build a movement of our own.
That was the Jeffersonian Club movement,
when we tried to bring some real democracy into politics
and into the union at the same time.
This way we offended everyone.

They managed to get rid of me and kick me out of the mines.
When I was fired, everything shut down.
The whole valley shut down.
All the big wheels from the union, they came out there
and called mass meetings.
They came to me and said, "Ted,
you tell the guys to get back to work
and we'll take your case.
After all, you were fired for being involved in union activity
and you'll get paid for every day you were off."

One Polish fellow, he started crying,
he said, "Ted, don't nail yourself to the cross.
When they try to nail you, you fight like hell,
but don't do it to yourself."

I was foolish enough to tell them to go back to work
and that was it.

My case is still pending. It never came up.
That was in 1936.
If I get paid for all those back wages,
I'll have it made.

I worked until they retired me.
When they retired me, it took three Coal and Iron police,
one at each arm and one at the seat of the pants.

They set me out into the middle of the road.

≈

III. GOD

In the days when they were first starting to build unions
and a child sees their dad just trying to be a free-spoken person
and he was fired out of this mine
and fired out of that mine
and you move from one community to another
until you get another job again
and that kid grows up in that environment,
seeing all those things that go on.
He sees the management as they go to church
in these nice white wagons
and sit in the front row.
Poor old Charlie Knocker, he goes
and he has to sit in the back row.

The kid sees this, and it makes him angry at the whole system.
He sees religion as something used to keep people in subjection.
He sees that there is no truth there, no honesty,
so he says, "To hell with the whole thing."
Righteous people looking at the kid will say he's going to hell.
But God will give that kid a chance.

❧

My brother Paul was raised during a time when the mine was new.
He went to work during a time when people were coming from Europe.
The company would send recruiters over to Europe,
usually someone who could speak the language.
The company would pay his way back to his country
to recruit men. They were paid by the head
so they often didn't recruit the most stable of men.
They would go to the saloons and find enough men
to fill a crew to bring over.
Those recruits were not the best citizens of that country.

So, Paul was raised among these
when he first went to work in the mines.
There were things that happened to Paul, too,
during that time that corrupted him.
He never had a chance at coming at God's truth.

When our little daughter died,
she was an innocent.
Who was anyone to judge if my little girl would go to heaven?
A lot of truths about God only started coming through to me
at that time.

❧

IV. NEW YORK DAYS (1930s–1940s)

In my life I've always wondered why.
Why was I exposed to this or that or the other experience?
Why, just when I seemed to have it made
in a particular area,
would that door close and a new one open
in an entirely different field?
Why did I find myself involved in something
that was not of my own making
but seemingly had no beginning
and seemingly will have no end?

Would it interest you to know
that Langston Hughes once instructed a class
in a labor school of which I was a member?

If you know Langston Hughes
you have my permission to check with him
as to whether this story is so.
I would ask about it low-key
because he may not want it generally to be known
that he once instructed a class
that was under Communist jurisdiction.
But then again he might not mind at all.

The intent of his poems was to make people aware
that the world is not free.
Even though on the surface the slaves have been freed,
underneath the struggle goes on
of one class attempting to dominate the other
by subterfuge, by terror, or by open brutal force of arms.
All this to keep the working class, the producers,
the ants of the human world in their place.

How beautifully he brings this out
in his poem about Spain during the revolution.

In 1937, there were many volunteers
who went to Spain to fight the Fascists,
who joined the Abraham Lincoln Brigade,
who came from the ranks of labor in the Pittsburgh district.
Six from the Russellton-Curtisville Valley.
Two of them returned, but four of them died.

I was the district secretary of the International Workers Order.
As the district secretary, I was instrumental in raising the money
to purchase three ambulances for the Abraham Lincoln Brigade
and enough money to furnish the ambulances
with surgical instruments and supplies.

The International Workers Order was the insurance wing
of the militant labor movement.

In 1938 the IWO ran a school for district class members
to learn about mortality tables and other actuarial tables.
The school was held in New York City in the old Broadway Hotel.
One of our instructors was the author of a book,
"Investing in Disaster."

The disaster part entered in
when the insurance companies devised a scheme
to combine insurance with savings,
in which, actually, a person became his own insurer.
But the worst part was that the insurance companies
became bankers.

The insurance companies had millions of dollars
of other people's money to invest.
The insurance companies' money was invested
in the companies that were the most brutal
in their suppression of labor
and legal and illegal interference
in any attempt of labor to organize.

I was not convinced that the insurance companies
were a boon to policyholders
or to the general public,
because they invested in industry.
That was why the IWO was organized,
to give the poor good insurance
at a rate they could afford,
where they were given an opportunity
to express their frustration.

The class was instructed to give an analytical report.
I made the report.

I'm not sure now if Mr. Hughes was then in the audience.
I'm assuming that he was, because the next day,
a Black man sat with me for a while,
gave me a package and left.
In the package was Langston Hughes' book of poems.

❧

After one class, a very kindly Black woman
questioned me about my background—
company camps, company money, Coal & Iron Police,
my parents' background and far back into history.

Before the day was over, a letter was given to me.
It read, "The only position or opinion of any value
is one you will die for. Hang in there
and don't cave in," signed, Paul Robeson.

The next day this beautiful, very kindly
woman spoke to our class.
She spoke softly about the feelings
of those looked down upon and discriminated against
through no fault of their own.
They had to do one of two things:
cave in and become cowering Uncle Toms,
or they rose to their full height of dignity,
lifting their voices like trumpets
to point to the sins of the oppressors
even if they had to die for it.

I sat there in tears, unable
to even stand as she left.

One of my classmates, a
girl from Wheeling, West Virginia,
said, "Wasn't she wonderful?
Especially when she said 'never bow down
to the people who have the stench
of the slave market on their clothes,
regardless of their words.'"

Then she told me that the woman was Marian Anderson.

That has now been 42 years ago.
At graduation, six places were named.
I didn't get any of them, but I did get a mention.
It was: "Mr. Gall is the one most likely to succeed."

Of course, it's still not too late for that.
I see that the roughest days of my life
and of all those now living
are just ahead.

❧

NOTES ON THE POEMS

The Miners' Strike of 1927–28: For more information, see R.S. Sukle's *Miner Injustice: The Ragman's War*, available on *Amazon.com*.

Coal and Iron Police: A private police force in the state of Pennsylvania, appointed by the governor but paid by the coal companies. Officially, the police existed to protect company property, but in practice the companies used them as strikebreakers and to coerce workers. Made up of men recruited from street gangs and prisons, they regularly and violently abused their power over the mining families.

Jefferson Clubs: Grassroots political clubs that promoted Jeffersonian ideals of democracy and community engagement in politics by educating working-class voters and organizing campaigns. They were instrumental in mobilizing support for Roosevelt, and endorsed his New Deal programs—Social Security, public works projects, and labor protections—as compatible with their vision of working toward the common good and protecting individual freedoms from the excesses of corporate power.

International Workers Order (IWO): The IWO was founded in 1930 and brought together diverse immigrant fraternal associations from across the U.S. to provide low-cost health insurance, educational programs, and social and cultural activities for workers and their families. Ted Gall was a prominent figure in the IWO and served as a district secretary in 1938—managing membership, organizing community events, and coordinating educational and cultural programs, in cooperation with local working-class communities, unions, and other left-wing organizations. Although most of its members did not belong to the Communist Party USA, the IWO's politics and leadership were aligned with those of the Party. During the "Red Scare" of the 1950's, the organization's insurance funds and records were seized by New York State's Insurance Department and the IWO was legally disbanded.

Labor School: IWO schools in Pittsburgh and New York City offered political and cultural education for workers. The schools had a significant impact on the lives of their students, shaping a generation of leftist intellectuals and labor activists. During the 1930's, the Workers School in New York City provided training to workers, labor organizers, intellectuals, and party members; it also offered language instruction for immigrants and classes in literature, theater, and music. Many artists and writers associated with the Harlem Renaissance and the New York intellectual left were involved with or taught at the school.

Langston Hughes: A world-renowned African American poet, social activist, novelist, playwright, and columnist from Joplin, Missouri. One of the earliest innovators of the literary art form called jazz poetry, Hughes is best known as a leader of the Harlem Renaissance.

Paul Robeson: An African American athlete, singer, actor, and activist. He rose to fame during a time when segregation was legal in the United States and Black people were being lynched by racist mobs in the South. A brilliant scholar of languages and world cultures, Robeson spoke more than 20 languages and became an advocate for the civil rights of people around the world.

Marian Anderson: An African American opera singer considered the greatest contralto of her time, and an icon of the civil rights movement. When the Daughters of the American Revolution denied her access to Constitution Hall because of her skin color, she instead sang from the steps of the Lincoln Memorial for a crowd estimated at 75,000. She traveled the world as a goodwill ambassador for the US.

Abraham Lincoln Brigade: A group of volunteers from the United States, many of them leftists, who fought in the Spanish Civil War in the 1930's. They served as soldiers, technicians, medical personnel, and aviators on the side of the Spanish Republican forces against the Nazi-supported forces of General Francisco Franco and his Nationalist faction.

AUTHOR'S NOTE

I hesitate to call myself the author of this poem, which was drawn exclusively from testimony Ted Gall left for his daughter, Suzanne Gall Sukle, who shared her father's archive with me. I didn't so much write the poem as compose it, choosing excerpts from his writing and shaping them into lines and stanzas. All the words—save two or three—are the words of Ted Gall, a man I wish I'd known. He created the archive he left for his daughter with a very clear eye toward history, so she and I are confident that he meant these words to be shared, and his story.

Ted Gall was born in 1905 and raised on a farm in Russellton, Pennsylvania. He started working in the nearby coal mines at the age of 12; several months later he began driving the delivery truck for the company store. He was in Russellton for the biggest miners' strike in history, in 1927–1928—when my paternal grandmother was also in Russellton, and my then-three-year-old father. Suzanne is sure that her father knew my grandmother, and I like to think that Ted Gall was the kind of man who shaped my father's character.

Russellton became what was called "a bucket of blood" for the violence that erupted there during the strike. By the time the strike had been crushed by the coal company and the state of Pennsylvania, Ted Gall had become radicalized. He joined the Communist Party USA (as did my paternal grandmother) and rose through the ranks of the International Workers' Order. After the leadership of the CPUSA was infiltrated by those he referred to as "Stalinist types," he tried to leave the party, but was drawn back into the fold by his commitment to the Civil Rights movement, which was supported by the CPUSA, and by his outraged sense of the injustices built into the American system. He finally managed to leave the party in the early 1950s, and then, with both the KGB and the FBI pursuing him, he was forced to go into hiding for several years.

Suzanne Sukle grew up hearing her father's stories, and he left her his archive in his will—journals and essays and speeches he composed; un-mailed letters he'd written to her; audiotapes—all meticulously organized. And then there was his file from the FBI: Ted Gall requested the file and waited five years for it to arrive; it came in the mail two weeks after his death. Suzanne has crafted the stuff of her father's life into two novels that I highly recommend: *Miner Justice: The Ragman's War* and *Blood on the Constitution*. Her research into her family's history and the history of labor in the U.S. has been a boon to my own research, and a blessing. I'm grateful for her generosity, her friendship, her fearlessness, and her wise and gentle guidance.

Excerpts from *LABOR: The Testimony of Ted Gall* first appeared in the online journal *Good River Review*.

EPIGRAPH

Remembering my father, Ted Gall,
An indomitable fighter for justice,
Unwavering advocate for labor equity,
Who fearlessly challenged power,
Leaving me a legacy of activism,
And a treasure trove of untold tales,
That guide me along a path of inquiry toward understanding
And inspire me to share the stories of courage and resilience.

Suzanne Gall Sukle

ABOUT THE AUTHOR

Cecilia Woloch is the author of a novel and six previous collections of poems, most recently an expanded and updated edition of *Tsigan: The Gypsy Poem*, which has been given multi-lingual, multi-media performances in Los Angeles, Paris, Warsaw, Athens and elsewhere; a poem from the new edition was also included in a memorial exhibit at Auschwitz-Birkenau in 2020. Her honors include fellowships from the National Endowment for the Arts, the Fulbright Foundation, CEC/ArtsLink International and the Center for International Theatre Development, as well as a Pushcart Prize and inclusion in The Best American Poetry series. Her work has been published in translation in French, German, Polish, Bulgarian, Hungarian, Ukrainian, Hebrew and Romanes. She collaborates regularly with musicians, dancers, visual artists, actors, and filmmakers. Born in Pennsylvania and raised in rural Kentucky, she has traveled the world as a teacher and writer.

www.ingramcontent.com/pod-product-compliance
Lightning Source LLC
Chambersburg PA
CBHW031241120626
46545CB00003B/1226